MURDER IN THE MARKET

Also by Maureen Thorpe

The Annie and Rosamund Series

Tangle of Time
Sailing to Byzantium
Coventina's Well

Maureen Thorpe

MURDER IN THE MARKET
or
(Death by pickle jar)

MAUREEN THORPE

Cover Design: Marius Hoofd and Shawn Wernig, Eggplant Studios
Author photo: kimberleyrae

Published in 2022 by:
Stone Circle Books
2410 Alpine Rd
Windermere, B.C. Canada V0B 2L2

LIBRARY AND ARCHIVES CANADA CATALOGUING IN PUBLICATION

Title: Murder In The Market / Maureen Thorpe Names: Thorpe, Maureen, author
Identifiers:Canadiana (print)
soft cover: 978-1-7779804-0-5
e-book: 978-1-7779804-1-2
Subjects: Mystery/Paranormal/Humour

The setting for this book is real. The story is fiction

Printed and bound in Canada

For the Organizers, Traders
and Patrons of all Farmers' Markets

It is hard to imagine a

civilization without onions

Juliet Child

Chapter 1

I wish to state that I have changed peoples' names to protect the innocent and more importantly, to prevent them from suing me for character assassination, although given where I am, suing me could prove difficult.

Every Saturday from June to September, my husband; Jay and I drag ourselves out of bed at 6 am and drive into our small mountain town in British Columbia to the Farmers' and Artisans' Market, which is organized by our branch of the Royal Canadian Legion and our Municipal District. Do please note: we are not weather dependent, so rain or shine, wind or storm, the market goes on, except for one instance I will mention below.

It is always an amazing sight to see an empty parking lot transformed into a village for four hours. We usually arrive before 8 am and by then most people have put up their pop-up tents and are arranging their various shelving and other inventive display paraphernalia. Chaos reigns but it's mainly organized chaos.

Let me digress for a moment. Whoever came up with the name 'pop-up tent' should be made to pop them up continuously for 72 hours straight. Pop-up tents do not pop up. It takes at least two people, if not four, to raise the damn things, in our case, at least four people as our pop-up is as ancient as we are.

Now that is not a problem as this temporary village is a community of warm like-minded souls who reach out to help each other on every occasion—all except one individual, with whom I have my own special and private beef. I'll come back to that individual. Right now, I want to enjoy the feeling of being part of my Saturday social group.

On this particular Saturday—I am oblivious as to how special it is going to be—our pop-up is miraculously up, my table unfolded and my books on display. (I am an author by the way; I write murder mysteries). The market is not yet open, so I chat with my next-door neighbour. She is an attractive woman; I will describe her as in her prime. She designs and makes the clothes she sells, not only that, she has created an intricate tube system, which she builds as she sits on the ground like an industrious garden gnome and, hey presto, she has a change room complete with a mirror. People flock around her stall like bees around a bee-hive. Don't get me wrong; I'm not jealous of the fact that she does so well, not really.

I wave across to Sandra. She sells honey and is just as sweet. She and her husband operate a honey farm up the valley. Can you have a honey farm or is it a bee farm? Next to her is Lavender Woman. She sells a skin cream that smells of lavender fields. She always looks stunning which blows me away because I believe she lives in her car. Next to her is Mary, owner of a vineyard down the valley. As she sells wine from her vineyard and offers free samples, she is extremely popular. We also have another alcohol stall; where the traders market gin and vodka with great success. Their products contain exotic and herbal flavours and are distilled right here in our valley. The company won bigtime on Dens and Dragons or some such show. They offer free samples too; as one reviewer wrote, 'it's the only market I know where you can get tipsy.' Down and across from my stall is a man with a lovely smile who fries small donuts. He always has a long queue. The donut smell haunts me all morning as I watch visitors eating them. So cruel.

I don't think I mentioned the fact that I am originally from England, as is my next-door neighbour, the garden gnome, so when we chat, I become nostalgic. I'm feeling slightly off-balance today because I keep remembering how it was when I first came to Canada and couldn't find HP Sauce at the grocery store. You have to understand that if any English people living in England are autopsied—after death of course—HP Sauce will be found in their bloodstream. To this day I shudder when I remember the painful withdrawal symptoms.

Chapter 2

The market operates from 9 am to 1 pm and has its own rhythm. Visitors trickle in at first, then the main crowd begins to build from about 10 am. Patience is the key to being a market trader. That expression reminds me of a conversation from a few weeks ago. I mentioned to a friend that Jay and I are market traders. She looked puzzled and then said, "in stocks and bonds?"

Back to the patience comment. One never knows how the day will go, especially with books. Clothing, jewellery and food, yes, they are a given. Books, well, I figure that of the hundreds of people who pass through, maybe 2% are readers. I, however, have patience and, I may add modestly, tolerance amongst my many virtues.

Allow me to relate an incident that occurred a couple of weeks ago. Jay had gone to buy coffee and a muffin for me to keep my blood sugar level up before the market opens, otherwise I cease being such a nice person, and I wandered around saying good morning to my neighbours. The individual I mentioned earlier with whom I have a beef is George. That day, George's stall was kitty-corner to mine. He likes to can produce from his garden. "Keeps me out of mischief," he says. He often mentions his onion patch and how he likes to take the green shoots of the sprouting onions and dry them, which I think is very clever. George is generally quiet. He doesn't mix much with the other traders; you might not know he is there, most times.

He always has something different on his stall and I became excited when I saw rows of jars of pickled onions. So, what, you might ask? Well, pickled onions are like HP Sauce to an English person; they are part of our heritage and a God-given right.

When Jay arrived back with the coffee, I told him about the pickled onions. "Go buy some before they have all gone," I demanded.

Now, the next stall to George's that day belongs to Alena. Alena taught herself the art of silk printing and now silk prints her own designs. I must say; people are ingenious. It also means that Alena has a keen eye and doesn't miss much so I know she saw Jay approach George and ask for pickled onions. Perhaps, if need be, I can call her as a witness.

I must tell you that my husband is a market socialite. After he has helped set up my stall and brought me coffee, he takes off on his rounds to chat with everyone. He usually comes back loaded down with purchases he can't resist. Pies, peaches and plums are the most common. Once it was ten cobs of corn! When he arrives this time, he confirms that he did buy some pickled onions. Saliva floods into my mouth as I anticipate the first crunchy bite.

Sales are good that day and after packing up and heading home, I celebrate by cutting a huge chunk of cheese; pry open the pickle jar and select—a large pickled garlic clove. Imagine my disappointment. I grab the jar. No label. No hint that these are garlic cloves and not pickled onions.

I call my husband from the kitchen. When I tell him about the error, he laughs. Like Queen Victoria before me, I am not amused. We grow our own garlic. We probably have at least five pounds from this year's harvest plus what's left over from last year, but that is beside the point. If you buy pickled onions, you should receive pickled onions. Being a reasonable human being, I eventually calm down and eat my cheese pickle-less.

I have mentioned our warm and friendly market neighbours. We also have market supervisors. Tom and Dan walk around all morning with their clipboards, checking off something or other, maybe who's been naughty and who's been nice. They are the ones who keep the chaos level down at setting up and taking down time, maintain Covid regulations and remove dogs from the arena, along with their owners, I presume.

In the early morning, a week after my pickle and garlic incident, there is an uproar nearby. This is most unusual. Curse words float over the market. Later, my husband tells me George has parked in the wrong spot. On Fridays we are supposed to check the number on the space we are allocated. I'm always in the same place. For some reason, George is moved around every week. Well, he has set up his display in the usual spot of the man who sells knives with wood-carved handles. It doesn't come to blows apparently, which is good because George is no spring chicken, and peace descends once more as Tom and Dan sort everything out with their usual diplomacy.

Chapter 3

I briefly mentioned Covid regulations; all of the events I describe happen during the Pandemic. So, we all wear masks and have hand sanitizers on our tables and partitions between tents. I just want to say it's not easy to talk about your book plots when wearing a mask and standing the required distance apart from your potential buyer. We authors are made of stern stuff; however, and overcome all obstacles placed in our path.

One of the highlights of the day is when the Egg Lady makes her rounds. She sells egg, bacon and cheese on a bun for $4. Everybody watches in anticipation for the Egg Lady. She is a member of the Canadian Legion which runs the market along with the Municipality and is aware some people have travelled a long way to get here. She calls at every stall and it is quite disappointing if she sells out before she gets to you and you have to wait for the next batch.

George caused a ruckus one time as he jumped the queue and took an egg sandwich out of turn. The man and his son who sell wood-turned pepper mills had waited in anticipation and complained loudly when they witnessed George munching on their egg sandwich. George looked in danger of having the stolen egg sandwich thrust down his throat. The peppermill makers frequently help us set up our so-called pop-up tent and are not usually given to egg rage. The reaction of the woodturners illustrates how tempers can flare when one is deprived of an expected meal. That was a nasty moment when I reflect upon it. Dan and Tom had to work hard to calm the troubled waters.

Jay and I are amazed by the ingenuity of people and what they make to sell at the market. Allow me to take you down our lane. The lines of tents create two rows. At the bottom end of our avenue, a family sells lemonade and popcorn; although their products seem to attract every wasp in the valley, they do a vigorous trade. We haven't really come to know them as they are at the end of the row. Then comes our donut maker. Nearer to our stall are two displays of jewellery, which are always popular, with women examining and buying. At the adjacent stall a pleasant woman sells the most amazing Thai dumplings. I already mentioned the honey and wine makers. Although I smile and make nice, I never buy; I leave that to my husband.

Of course, it's not just the stall holders who are at the market; we have hundreds of visitors. Ours is a destination town and the market relies on all of these visitors to visit and empty their pockets. Mainly though, they empty their pockets to buy food. Whether it be giant pretzels or sugar juice poured over ice, or donuts, the visitors are constantly eating. I *can* guarantee they won't be eating pickled onions.

I love people watching. I pride myself on spotting readers. I can tell by the way their eyes drift to my stall. Non-readers stare straight ahead as though I'm selling religious texts or asking for donations to our curling rink. I like to stand in front of my stall, book in hand. When I ask passers-by what they like to read, the answer, eight times out of ten is, "nothing, I don't read," or, just as often, the answer is a blank stare. Readers come straight to the stall, eyes shining and ready to listen. Not that any of this has anything to do with what happened but

I'm just trying to give you a flavour of our happy camp.

There is an osprey nest in the trees above the parking lot; they are fun to watch when I'm standing there alone with no buyers. When I'm osprey-watching, I often see the same man walking along the brow of the hill across from us, always at the same time, mid-morning. He seems to take a particular interest in the market, looking down at it from his lofty perch, very much as the ospreys do. He is silhouetted against the sky-line, has a beard and always carries a paddle. He is probably a local but I don't recognize him.

Talking of our visitors—and I am not judgmental, not at all––I have never seen so many tattoos. I swear there is no un-inked skin left in the Western Hemisphere. Years ago, I took a university Anthology course called 'Bodies in the Pacific'. It was all about the tradition of the Māori people painting their bodies with tattoos and the beliefs behind it. Fascinating. But this modern compulsion—well, it's nothing to do with me and as I said, I am certainly not judgmental so I'll keep my mouth shut.

I mentioned weather. Weather is crucial to our wonderful market. Sunshine is perfect unless you have baked goods and you can't find shade. The real enemy is wind. I remember last year when a wind came out of nowhere and tents that weren't weighted down flew into the air like a multitude of Mary Poppins. The market ended abruptly. We all learned from that and now everyone has weights for the so-called pop-up tents. The rain has been scarce this year, but I remember a heavy rain last year. I invited visitors to shelter under my tent. We were like the proverbial sardines but chattier. Unfortunately, no one bought a book as a result of my generous hospitality.

This year we have had to cope with smoke drifting in from forest fires. Believe it or not, on this particular morning there is ash on our car. Ash! We know there are no fires close by so these particles of burning trees have come to us from across the mountains. The sun, as it rises above the opposite range of mountains, is dark red; the reddest I have ever seen. As we drive into town, I watch it. I keep watching it as it rises higher. It has created such an eerie atmosphere as if Armageddon has arrived. The air is so smoky; the sun remains red even as it climbs higher.

Maybe that's why I feel so discombobulated, as though I am

leaning slightly instead of being upright. The feeling makes me think of a ship listing to port or starboard, whichever. I think the problem is that I haven't had my egg sandwich yet. I can feel my blood sugar dropping. I kid you not. Ask anyone with this problem. I am turning into a werewolf.

Jay has taken off on his travels. I'm still waiting for some form of sustenance and standing in front of my stall as I anticipate the magical 9 am, which is the time Tom and Dan open the barriers and spray peoples' hands and tell them they can only walk one way around the market—Covid rules. This is the time I always experience collywobbles. What will this day bring in terms of sales? My focus sharpens and I prepare to go on stage.

Chapter 4

Today, for some reason I am not anxious. I stare dully up the avenue made by the tents; there are no people yet although I can see the queue beyond the Covid-induced barrier. I can't do this anymore. I have to get out. I have a tight feeling in my chest and, it is preventing me from breathing. I must go for a walk.

The red sun is at my back; I feel its presence through my shirt. Its heat is burning a hole right between my shoulder blades. I make my way toward the public washroom. I can splash water on my face in there.

The traders are quiet. The red sun has created a sense of oppression. There is no chatter, no laughter. I am bewildered. This is not my market, not my social place.

Two stalls before the washroom, I see George's neat rows of canned jars. I can't yet see George because all of the tents have side and back panels—Covid rules. Hesitantly, I waver between carrying on and stopping, then driven by what, I do not know, I walk up to his stall and look in. There he is, sitting at the back, reading.

"Hello, George," I say. Even to my ears, my voice sounds tight and strained. It must be the damn smoke. I step behind his table. Now, *this* is not market etiquette. He hasn't invited me and we are not exactly friends. I reach for one of his jars of garlic cloves. Still. No. Label.

"George," I say. "Have you ever thought of labelling your jars?"

"I always do," says he, "but not the garlic. Anyone who's not an idiot can see they are garlic cloves."

I can see the red sun in my mind's eye. The redness spreads. I watch my arm swing forward. The jar is still in my hand. It lands on George's white thatch of hair. The metal rim of the jar buckles, the seal is broken and the glass shatters into a thousand pieces, sending garlic cloves, tiny fragments of glass and liquid all over both of us. I curse and attempt to wipe the juice off my clothes. That's when I realize George is not sitting in his chair. He's lying on the ground.

"George," I say. "George, get up, you silly old fool. Look what you've done to me. I stink of your damn garlic."

George does not get up. He does not move. His eyes stare glassily at me. I can see he, too, is covered in garlic juice and minute glass splinters, but there is no blood. I shake my head. What happened? Did he choke on a clove? He couldn't have drowned; there wasn't that much juice. I look out of the tent. Nothing. No visitors yet. Stall holders appear to be huddled at the back of their tents reading or contemplating their navels. I look frantically around the stall. My brain has disconnected from my body—almost. I bend down and begin to push George underneath his draped table. I am amazed he is so light, almost skin and bone. When I can't see him anymore, I stand; God, my back is killing me.

The prudent thing is to act normally. Don't forget, I write murder mysteries. I am an expert on murder. All will be well. I walk out of the back of the tent—clever thinking, right—and make my way back to my stall by remaining close to the stone wall that denotes the end of the parking lot and separates it from the hill behind. My path leads behind the other tents and vehicles.

I arrive at my stall with a sigh of relief just before Jay returns with, as usual, bags filled with his treasures.

"You look different," he says. "Your face is bright red and, wow, you smell like an Italian Restaurant and why have you put on your coat?"

"I'm cold. I've just been to the bathroom," I say, "and I will ignore your rudeness. We had pasta last evening for dinner, remember. Where are my muffin and coffee? What took you so long?" I prepare to meet my public as I quickly devour a muffin.

Chapter 5

The morning progresses. Jay is next door chatting to the garden gnome as he does when she has no customers, which isn't often. I strain to hear their conversation through the flimsy barrier; not that I don't trust Jay, not for a minute, but who knows how the garden gnome behaves.

I sell my first book. Now I know I'm golden. The world has stopped teetering and I am standing upright. I sell two more books. I have to do a lot of talking as people always say, "what are your books about?" This always blows me away. I mean, if you sell, say pickled onions and you have a huge sign that says 'pickled onions for sale', you don't expect people to say, "do you sell pickled onions." I have signs plastered all over saying 'murder mysteries' but everyone still says "what are your books about?" C'est la vie. I battle on.

Jay returns from another of his walkabouts including another chat with the garden gnome. He waits until I have finished with another customer—business is picking up.

"You won't believe this," he says. Now *his* face is red.

How do I know I won't believe it—I haven't heard what he has to say yet. Probably someone sold him some mushy strawberries. They have been terrible this year; it must be due to the heat and smoke.

"Are you listening?"

"Yes," I lie.

"The Egg Lady went to that guy George's stall to make sure he got his egg sandwich; you know how he makes such a fuss about it. Well, she couldn't see him, so she asked his neighbours. They hadn't seen him either…"

I begin to catch the drift of what he is saying.

"… so, she went into the stall calling his name and saw a foot sticking out from under the cloth on his table."

I feel a chill.

"She screamed and the man next door; he sells those pottery mugs—"

I almost scream.

"Well, he's dead."

"Sounds like a heart attack," say I. "He was getting on a bit."

"Tom and Dan have sent for the RCMP," Jay continued.

My chill deepens. "I would have thought a doctor might be more appropriate."

"There's not much a doctor can do if he's dead," my husband comments in what I know he considers a reasonable voice.

"May I remind you that I am the expert on murder," I say. "I mean, writing about it. Someone has to pronounce him dead and then an autopsy will find he died of natural causes."

"We don't know that though, do we? Maybe someone hit him over the head. He did annoy quite a few people, including you, come to think of it."

"Oh, well done, fitting me up for a murder, are you? You know I wouldn't hurt a soul. I can't even bear killing spiders. So don't mention that to anyone. People get funny ideas."

A customer comes along at that point in the conversation, which is probably a good thing. She is one of my regulars and looks like the bearer of news.

"Have you heard the news?" she whispers—predictably. "George, that old guy who sells the canned stuff, is dead. Not the other couple who sell canned stuff: the fella on his own. The Egg Lady found him. She's being treated for shock at the hospital. The RCMP have just arrived with one of the doctors from the clinic; the clinic on the main street, not the one on the other street."

God help me who cares which clinic. "Has the doctor examined him yet," I ask, attempting to sound curious rather than anxious.

"No. The police are busy sealing off the tent—George's tent, I mean, and somebody said they are sealing off the whole parking lot, with all these people in it too. Isn't it exciting? Why are you wearing your coat? It's hot out here now. I can see you're sweating."

"I'm cool in the shade of the tent," I say. I realize now that the coat isn't as much masking the smell of garlic as amplifying it.

"I want to buy your latest book," she says, "and can you

sign it with the date and put that it's the date of George's murder. That's going to look great in a murder book and will increase the value."

I look at her appalled. "It could be natural causes you know and, seriously, that's a gruesome idea." Still, a sale is a sale so I dutifully do as she asks but I put 'death' not 'murder'. Really.

I take my chair back into the shade of the tent next to Jay. I always sit outside the stall so I can prepare for the next glinty-eyed reader but I have a feeling that sales have dried up today. Too bad, I enjoyed a booming business for a while.

I share the latest news with Jay. "They are erecting one of those tents like you see on T.V. A doctor has arrived along with the RCMP."

At that moment, Tom appears in front of our stall. "Orders from the police. Please remain inside your tent and no more sales today. I guess you've heard, we have a casualty."

"In that case, I'll close my eyes for a while," says Jay. Head back, he's out like a light. Trapped inside our Covid protected space, I can see out but people are no longer moving up and down the lane; they have formed clusters—not physically distanced I must say, and, amazingly, still eating, having lowered their masks temporarily. It reminds me of the many times I have tried to eat my muffin through my plastic faceguard. One feels such a fool.

Anyway, there we sit. I move my chair to the far-right side of the tent. Now I can see up the avenue, not clearly though as visitors block the view. I can see the extra tent the officials have erected in front of George's shelter and people in white jump-suits moving in and out. I am frustrated. I only can catch glimpses of the operation as people stand like statues nearby, the police not yet having moved them on. The tent grows hotter as noon approaches and my garlic smell develops more pungency. I wake myself with a snort as an RCMP officer pops his face around the corner making me jump. My husband remains undisturbed; he sleeps on.

"Good day, madam, sir." He looks at Jay, head back, mouth open, and clears his throat loudly. I poke Jay in the ribs with my elbow. That wakes him up soon enough.

"I expect you are wondering what is going on," said the officer who, to use a cliché, looks to be about twelve years old and sounds like a police instruction manual. "Sadly, we have incurred a casualty at the market. We await a preliminary report from the doctor before we can move the body, er, casualty. In the meantime, we are taking the names and addresses of everyone here, stallholders and visitors." Then, "Boy, you must have had an early lunch, smells like a pizza joint in here. Wouldn't mind a piece of pizza myself."

We dutifully give our names, phone number and address.

"Ah, locals, I see. You may be able to leave earlier, especially given your ages. We know where to find you." He smiles but there is menace behind those words; I can feel it. I didn't appreciate the crack about age either. I hate ageism. Did he think we/I are too old to commit murder?

I continue trying to catch glimpses of the activity up the avenue. At one point an ambulance is backed up to the recently erected white tent and a stretcher is loaded into it. I can see no details because of the crowd. It's time the police moved them out. I mean, really, what visitor is going to kill a trader, unless the bargaining becomes too heated.

When we are eventually permitted to pack up, Tom and Dan

are being about as tight-mouthed as an alligator with toothache; they share nothing. It is strangely quiet taking down the tents—just as awkward to take down as to pop-up, I might mention. The dismantling of the market is the slowest I have ever experienced. Normally, people are out of there like a shot but it is obvious that folks are lingering like drivers rubbernecking at an accident on the road. This is better than television.

We find out nothing more. We return home dispiritedly. I'm sure that my husband, Mister Sociability, might have been able to uncover more information had he tried instead of spending far too much time chatting with our attractive friend at the next tent. I bet the phones will be hot in town this evening. It will be interesting to see what the chatter is on Facebook.

Chapter 6

We wait and wait. Our local paper reports only that a casualty had been found at the market. The word 'body' has been removed from the narrative. The rumour mill has a field day. Only I know what had really happened and I'm not about to share that experience with anyone. It wasn't my fault anyway. The stupid man should have. Labelled. His. Jars. And anyway, I didn't know the metal tops on those canning jars were so strong *and* the red sun had some sort of effect on my reasoning *and* I hadn't eaten.

I anticipate a phone call every day; the tension quite interferes with the flow of my writing. Two days later the call arrives: please attend the police station for routine fingerprinting at 2 pm tomorrow.

When we arrive, I see a whole line of people standing outside the station, all there for the same reason, I presume, with masks in place and socially distanced. I recognize many of them as our market colleagues. Some must have had quite a drive. How inconvenient for everyone. An officious woman makes sure we obey the Covid rules.

Lots of chatter is going on. Who, what, where, et cetera.

"This will eliminate us from inquiries," some know-it-all says.

I'm not worried. The only object I handled was the jar and it shattered. I don't know how they could find a whole print on those glass fragments. I had also brushed, stripped and washed all of my clothes, using bleach in the washing machine water. Let them try to find garlic on anything.

When our turn arrives, Jay and I dutifully roll each finger and thumb as instructed. We have just wiped off the black inky stuff with tissues and are turning to leave when a police officer who is as tall as he is wide calls our names. "Could you please step into this room? I need to take a statement from you."

I remain calm. Jay is always calm. "Certainly," I say with a sweet smile. "How is the case proceeding, officer, any progress?"

Don't forget I'm a writer of murder mysteries; I know the drill.

There are no smiling eyes above his black mask. "I am one of the investigating officers at this station: Corporal James by name."

"Is this routine, Officer?" I say, frowning to show my displeasure.

"Absolutely," says he. "Just clearing up a few matters. Please give me an account of your actions last Saturday. I am, of course, referring to the morning of the market."

So, I recount my day last Saturday. How we set up our stupid so-called pop-up tent with help from neighbours. "They always help us," I say. "We are well-liked by the other stall-holders."

"Do continue," he says. Rather impatiently I think.

"Well, when the stall is arranged to my liking Jay goes for coffee and I usually go to the washroom. Get it out of the way, so to speak." I lower my head as though embarrassed to refer to bodily functions.

"And is that what you did last Saturday?"

"Yes," I say. "Then I went back to our stall and Jay arrived with the coffee and my muffin. I need it to maintain my blood sugar, you know."

"Is there any garlic in your muffin?" he asks.

Right out of the blue, just like that!

I blink. "What a silly thing to say. I'm sure the coffee shop doesn't put garlic in their muffins, do they, Jay?"

"No, of course not, but you did smell of garlic, remember, I commented?"

Idiot.

"And remember I reminded you we had pasta on Friday evening. The smell must have lingered." I glare at him.

That was it. Corporal James left and we were ushered out of the station.

Chapter 7

As the days pass I carry on with my writing, my conscience remains clear and untroubled. Jay, who often meets his friends in town for coffee, returns with no fresh news. George's death might never have happened. I had wondered if a request might be made for the clothing I had been wearing that Saturday, but the horse has bolted. I don't suppose they could ask everyone for their clothing now.

Saturday comes around again, as it always does, and we follow our usual routine, arriving at the market at 8 am and wrestling with our pop-up. Strangely, no one offers to help. There are no cheerful good mornings. Our neighbour the garden gnome sits as usual and assembles her dressing room. I look at her in the early morning light before the barriers are erected and revise my earlier estimate. Yes, she is definitely past her prime, by a long chalk, I think with satisfaction.

All of the regulars are here: the donut man, the jewellery makers, the honey honey and the wine seller. It is eerily quiet; no one looks up from their activity and when the market has arisen to become a village, everyone retreats to the back of their caves.

Tom and Dan do their rounds in silence. God only knows what they are writing on their clipboards today. There is no sign of our Egg Lady or any Egg Lady. We are to starve then. I force myself to make the journey to the washroom, my eyes firmly fixed on the ground. It is important to behave as normally as possible, but as no one else is either that's a plus for me. There is a coldness in the air and I don't mean the temperature; it's more like everyone is withdrawing from each other. Trust has vanished.

9 am strikes. Immediately my mind thinks of 'For Whom the Bell Tolls'; visitors begin to trickle in. It's amazing. I can actually sense their inquisitiveness, their greed to know more, their rubbernecking. I am disgusted, but I contain my revulsion and begin my pitch. Sales are sales. The show must go on.

I begin to notice RCMP officers amongst the crowds as the

morning progresses. They appear to be casually chatting to all and sundry, both stall-holders and visitors. No doubt they will arrive at our humble venue eventually.

Sure enough, a uniformed officer arrives at my table; I doubt he is there to buy a book.

"Good morning," he says. First good morning today, I might add. Jay is off on his walkabout after helping garden gnome to finish setting up.

"May we step inside for a few moments? I need to clarify some matters."

What can I say but, "yes, of course? I'll bring my chair inside. You may have Jay's chair." Be polite, be helpful.

"My name is Corporal Bouvard. The RCMP officer who first gave you the news of the, er, event last week, happened to mention your tent smelled of pizza. He suggested you may have had an early lunch. Do you recall that conversation?"

I sigh, deeply. "If you are referring to the twelve-year-old in uniform, yes I do. I have also explained that I had pasta the previous evening and may have overdone the garlic. We grow a lot of garlic and I have to use it up."

"I see. It's amazing that the smell lasted so long."

"I don't understand what the issue is here," I say. Other people must smell, why pick on me?"

"We have to rule out any irregularities, that's all, just routine. Thank you for your cooperation, it's appreciated," says Corporal Bouvard.

"Good riddance," I thought.

As he was making his way to the front of the table, he stopped. "When you left your tent did you stop to say good morning to George Freeman?"

I sighed again. "I have no memory of saying good morning to George Freeman. He wasn't one of my favourite people so why would I?"

As soon as I said that I could have bitten off my tongue.

"You and George didn't get along?" he asked. "Was there friction between you?"

I laughed. "No, our paths rarely crossed."

"Strange, because Peter Drake, he's the sketch artist here, thought he saw you go into George's tent but didn't see you come out."

"Then Peter is dreaming. He is always drawing, anyway. He doesn't even look up at customers so how he could have seen me is impossible. I only went to the washroom, perhaps he saw me then, walking by. Have you talked to the guy who makes the pepper grinders? He and George had a row the other week, quite nasty it was. His stall is just down there. And another thing; there's a man comes across the hill at the same time every Saturday. I always think he looks suspicious as he pays an inordinate amount of attention to the market and he carries a paddle, which would make a great weapon. He could easily have crept into the back of George's tent. I see a lot when I'm standing out front."

The Corporal nodded his head. "It's interesting that you believe a weapon was involved," he says as he leaves. I watch him move along the stalls. I'm content though, I believe I threw enough dust at other people to cloud the issue.

I use red herrings in my stories all the time. They work so well in providing misdirection. The brilliant part about using misdirection is that it's incredibly easy and it's amazing how distractable we are. To quote the policeman, it will be 'interesting' to see if he was misdirected.

Chapter 8

Life resumed its usual rhythm. No more calls come from the police station. I am free.

Saturdays roll around with their usual regularity. Market days come and go. The season is coming to a close; only a few more to go. Jay goes east on a two-week trip to see his family and me, well, I manage on my own, struggling to carry the heavy books to the car, struggling to unload the car, asking, nay, begging for help to put up the so-called pop-up.

A strange thing happens one Saturday morning. I am driving into town, pleased to notice that the smoke from which we have suffered all summer, has dissipated, (we have experienced a couple of heavy rainfalls at last). I hear something rolling around in my car. At first, I'm not alarmed as I keep my stall display equipment in the car all summer; it saves loading and unloading, only the books are packed and unpacked.

Bump, clatter, on it goes, but it sounds as though it is coming from beneath me at the front. I pull into Tim Hortons; the parking lot is jam-packed as usual. I can't find a parking spot so I pull out and carry on into town.

When I arrive at my stall as always, I stop the car. Now, Tom and Dan have a rule: remove your gear from your vehicle and drive away, leaving the lane clear for the next vehicle. I unload my equipment, struggling with the heavier stuff. No husband and no help, so strange, so different. I look everywhere for whatever is rolling around. Ah, I see the culprit. It's a jar of something. It must have been there from my last shopping trip having escaped from its bag. It is under the seat at the front. I reach in and retrieve it. I haven't missed anything from my last shopping expedition but it happens. Once it was a package of ground beef that had become a fugitive from bondage. That package eventually made its presence known; oh, my God, it was disgusting, maggots everywhere. Jay had to clean up that mess.

I look with curiosity at this jar. It's a canning jar. I don't remember buying any canned goods. I can my own. The outside of the jar is bare. No label. I peer at the contents. Jay, bless him, must have found me some pickled onions. No—I recognize them now—garlic cloves!

My legs turn to jelly and I look around. If this is someone's idea of a joke, it's not funny. I don't see anyone watching to view my reaction so I nonchalantly—as best I can with jelly legs—climb back into the car and drive away to find a parking spot. I dump the jar in a garbage can on the way back and carry on with my day.

It's not until I return home and am savouring an Australian Merlot that I realize what must have happened. Jay had bought two jars of so-called pickled onions from George and one has remained trapped under the seat all this time. I check the fridge; yes, the first one sits there. I have used the cloves in cooking—waste not, want not. My mother taught me that adage *ad infinitum*. My relief is overwhelming. How silly of me to react so strongly. Obviously no one knows anything about that day but me.

Chapter 9

Jay returns from Toronto. The market has finished and I forget all about thanking him for the second jar of garlic.

I always drive into town on Fridays to do my weekly shop. Late September is lovely; many of our visitors have gone so parking is easier and the grocery store is not so crowded. Covid is still with us so masks are required, so wearying, it goes on and on.

There is still lots of fresh fruit around and I am busily sorting peaches out in the grocery section when a cart catches my thigh. I turn sharply to berate the bad driver but he has quickly moved on. Interesting, from the back view, he reminds me of someone I know but I can't think who.

Life continues to be busy. I am in the process of preparing for a trip back to the U.K. I presume because the police have not contacted me, I am free to go. I still have family there, plus

I can indulge in—you guessed it, pickled onions accompanied by pork pie and HP sauce.

I am away for three weeks and probably have gained ten pounds. We are deep into the Fall when I return —known as Autumn in England. I have enjoyed seeing the oaks and sycamores change colour over there. We don't see a brilliant colour change in the mountains, although the larch's glorious yellow shines like a beacon amongst the dull green fir trees.

Jay and I decide to enjoy the Fall weather and go for a walk along one of the many trails around town; this togetherness is a rare event for us. A few people are out, enjoying the late sunshine. Jay is telling me a story about one of his mates in Toronto—see, I'm speaking English again after three weeks back home. By the way, did I tell you my husband is Canadian? He is my third husband and my toyboy really as he is much younger than I am. I have grown older gracefully, and can still hold my own against younger women.

Anyway, we are walking up a steep hill that curves around a corner. I am focused on breathing but cough as I inhale a strong smell of garlic.

I say, "Boy, can you smell that?"

"Smells like garlic, or maybe it's a skunk," Jay responds.

Thinking of garlic reminds me of George for some reason, which reminds me of pickled onions so I regale Jay with my fascinating stories of recent Ploughman's lunches and pints of beer.

Fall becomes winter, my least favourite season. I know everyone skis on our mountains or skates on our frozen lake and shares how amazing it all is on Facebook. Jay continues running. Did I share with you that he is a runner? He runs in all weathers. I, on the other hand, hibernate. I write while wearing layers of woolly clothing.

Jay is out running and I am sitting at my desk, my laptop humming along as I work on my next murder mystery. I am so focused on my writing that when the phone rings I jump out of my skin.

"Hello," I say.

"This is Purolator. We have a package for you."

I haven't ordered anything online so somebody has sent me something. It will be my birthday soon; perhaps it is a present. I abandon my writing and drive down the road to the Purolator office. It is a small package but heavy. I can't wait to get home and open it. No way I'm waiting for my birthday. I examine the wrapping paper; it is a standard Purolator package with no return address. I eventually find my scissors. Jay never puts them back where they belong. When I have the contents exposed, I sink to the floor with a cry—four jars of pickled garlic cloves.

Who is doing this to me? No one saw anything at the market, I'm sure. I know people behaved differently after the, er, event but that was because they were all shocked.

I daren't show the jars to Jay; he may become too curious. He's never mentioned the garlic smell again as he soon moves on to whatever he is doing next. What can I do with them? Where can I hide them? I know; I'll empty the garlic cloves into the garbage bin. No, I can't do that, he'll smell them. I'll put them on the compost heap. No, he'll see my footprints in the snow. In frustration, I begin to cry. Finally, I empty the cloves into our in-house compost bin and, putting on my boots, trudge out to the compost heap and dump them. I use the compost fork to cover them with leaves. I wash the jars and add them to my collection in the back storage room. I scrub out the compost bin.

The first thing Jay says when he returns is, “wow, have you been making pasta sauce? I can really smell the garlic.”

Chapter 10

That night, I dream of George. Well, I think it is George. I can't remember what he looks like but he is standing at the end of the bed smiling at me and shaking his finger. I sit up in bed with a cry that actually awakens Jay. It takes a lot to do that.

"Whatsthematter," he mumbles.

I'm shaking and crying. "I had a nightmare, I think. Put the light on, Jay." The bedside light illuminates the room. There is no one there. I'm not sure though so I insist Jay checks the whole house for invaders. He mutters as he gets back into bed, shivering now. "I think you're losing it," he says and rolls over to go back to sleep. I yell when he puts his cold feet on mine and kick them off.

I can't write anymore. I stare at the blank screen and smell garlic. I dream about garlic most nights. It's no longer growing in the veggie garden as Jay has harvested the crop but I imagine the same scene everytime I walk past; the garlic scapes writhe out of the chain-link fence and wrap themselves around me. I am living in the nightmare of 'The Day of The Triffids' by John Wyndham. I move into the spare bedroom so my tossing and turning doesn't alert Jay to the fact that I am going crazy.

Now we are into February. There have been no more parcels, thank God. I still have no idea who could have sent them but it has to be someone *who knows*. What really scares me is that if someone knows, what are they waiting for? What do they plan to do next?

My publisher is after me to fulfil my contract: fat chance. He can whistle Dixie as far as I am concerned. My writing days are over. I'll have to pay back my advance. Who cares?

I still have to shop for food; Jay refuses to take on that job. He has enough to do, he says. I mean really; he shovels snow, big deal. I dread going out. I wear my big winter coat with a fur hood and wrap myself in scarves. Once I add my mask I will never be recognized. Not that I care. I have been a recluse since all of this happened except for grocery shopping yet have not received one phone call or text from anyone. I am forgotten, lost in the wilderness of my own pain. You may say the pain is of my own making, but I will say again: it was his fault. He. Should. Have. Labelled. The. Jars.

I am in the lineup with my groceries. I must resemble a miniature panda (I am not tall). We have designated circles to stand on—Covid rules. A man walks through the space ahead of me, pushing his cart. He turns and smiles. It's George.

I collapse onto the ground screaming.

Chapter 11

I wake up in the hospital, sans coat, sans scarves, sans boots and mask and when I check, sans clothes. I am wearing a hospital gown. I'm bewildered. A nurse comes around the corner of the privacy curtain. She is masked. I don't recognize her.

"Well, dearie—"

Dearie. OMG.

"You did have quite a turn in the grocery store. The staff sent for Dr. Solomon. He had to come and give you a shot as you wouldn't stop screaming. You're in emerg. now. Have you ever had that happen to you before?"

I stare at her as best I can. I am also sans my glasses. "Where are my glasses?" I demand.

She reaches over to a bedside locker and retrieves my glasses, carefully trying to place them on the bridge of my nose. I snatch them from her.

"I'm perfectly capable of putting on my own glasses, thank you."

"Sorry, dear. Only trying to help."

"Do you have my name written on a chart somewhere?"

"Yes, dear. We found the information in your wallet, including your health card. We have notified your husband that you are here. Well, I think the receptionist left a message as he didn't answer. Your purse is safe and sound in this locker."

"Then use my name," I snap. "I am not your dearie and where are my clothes and why did someone remove them without my permission."

I see her back stiffen. If there was a smile under her mask, it has disappeared. "We had to remove your clothes because they were, er," she cleared her throat, "soiled."

"Soiled," I almost scream. (I've had lots of practice in the screaming department lately). Soiled with what?"

"I'm afraid you emptied your bladder."

I could not believe my ears. I bet she enjoyed saying that too.

"Our doctor on call is Dr. Solomon. You met him already. He will be along to examine you once the lab has taken some blood."

"I do not need any blood taken; I just want to go home. Phone my husband and tell him to come and get me now and bring fresh clothes."

"I'm afraid I can't do that. Doctor's orders, you know. Try to rest." She disappeared.

I am livid. She had treated me like an old woman with Alzheimer's whereas I'm almost a famous author. Once I take a few deep breaths and calm down to simmer point, I try to remember what had happened in the grocery store. George, I saw George. Or did I? I see George everywhere now, so it seems. I think my mind must be playing tricks. I must get used to it. I can't afford to make a habit of ending up in the hospital all the time.

Another head appears around the curtain. "Ah, there you are."

Seriously, what is the matter with these people? Where else would I be? They put me here.

I grunt.

"Hello again. You are looking much better than the last time

I saw you, So, can you tell me what happened to you in the grocery store? Take your time, dear."

Unbelievable. I take a deep breath. "My *dear* doctor, I have no idea what happened to me. Maybe it happened because I had to wait so long on my little Covid circle."

Dr. Solomon smiles uncertainly. "You do have a way with words," he says with a small laugh.

"I should," I say, glaring at him. "I am almost a famous author."

"How interesting. What do you write?"

"Murder mysteries," I snarl.

"How nice. I'm just going to listen to your heart and perform a few neurological tests. When we get the results back from your blood work, we'll have a better idea of what might have caused the attack." He moved toward me, removing his stethoscope from his pocket.

"I haven't had any blood work yet," I say, "and there isn't a problem."

"The lab tech will be here as soon as she can," he murmurs as though to placate me.

Suffice it to say I allow him to examine me. I apparently have no choice. I had not realized I live in a dictatorship.

When he left, a young woman, I should say girl—about as old as that policeman at the market—pops her head around the curtain. "Hello," she says, "I've come to take some blood."

At least she didn't call me dearie.

"Do you really require that much?" I say as I watch my life's blood draining into those glass vial things?

She fiddles with her equipment and leaves. That was that. Now all I have to do is wait.

At last, Dr. Solomon returns to inform me of his results. "You are as healthy as a seventy-year-old can be," he says with a cheerful grin. "You may go home and write away. There is just one little thing." He pauses. "Your blood pressure is quite high. I wonder, are you experiencing any unusual stress, stress being such a deadly enemy? It may even have brought on your attack at the store.

Anyway, I have sent a note to your doctor. She will follow up. Apparently, your husband is not yet home. We did leave a message. Can anyone else who can pick you up?"

"No," I answer and turn away from him.

My beloved husband eventually turns up about four hours later. "I didn't see the message on the phone," he says. He uses the landline rather than a cell phone. I dress in silence and we leave.

Chapter 12

I lay awake in bed that night, recapping the day's events. I know that man I saw in the store was George. I had a good look at his face and he smiled in exactly the same way as he occasionally did at the market. What does that tell me?

He didn't die. It's the only conclusion to which I can come. He didn't die. I did not kill him. Not, of course, that I intended to. Logically, therefore, *he* is the one taunting me with the jars of garlic. I feel much relieved although I haven't forgiven my husband for making me wait so long at the hospital. He didn't see the message on the phone. Really. Didn't he notice I had been missing for about seven hours when he knew I had only gone grocery shopping? He must be losing his marbles. He may be a few years younger than I, but obviously, his mind is unravelling.

Tomorrow, I will begin writing again and my life will return to normal.

Chapter 13

I'm so happy. I sit down at my desk and switch on my laptop for the first time in months. I pick up where I had left off. The words flow easily. I write 1000 words by noon.

I make an appointment with my hairdresser for a long-neglected cut and colour. My grey roots are at least three inches long and the style has vanished. I am amazed when the receptionist tells me the first opening will be in two weeks. I can see, looking in the mirror that I have let myself go. Understandable under the circumstances. No wonder my blood pressure is high.

I decide to go the whole way and book a spa treatment. A spa is such an indulgence and the treatments will bring a glow back to my skin. I search the house for Jay to tell him I am feeling much better and think I may return to the connubial bed. He is nowhere to be seen. Out on a run, I guess.

I decide to drive down and pick up the mail at our community box. I had ordered more books a few weeks before, maybe they had been delivered, if not I would check at the post office. The mailbox is empty except for the usual flyers. I smile to myself. At least there are no boxes filled with garlic cloves.

I drive into town. The roads are still slushy as it's only March and dirty-looking snow is piled at the sides of the road. People are walking up and down the main street in brightly coloured down coats, all looking like clones so the coats must be this year's fashion statement. There is some heat in the sun though when it shows. Spring must be coming soon. Thoughts of the sun reminds me of the red sun last summer. For a second, I shudder; my newly found peace wobbles.

Covid is still ever-present, so on entering the lobby of the post office, I don my mask. Only five people are allowed in the lobby at one time; social distancing is rigorously followed. There are rumours of a vaccine on the horizon, fingers crossed. Luckily, only three people are lining up so I won't have to stand outside in the cold.

We nod at each other as I take my place in the line-up. Who

is who? Masks provide the perfect disguise anyway; think of bank robbers. The outside door opens and a cold draught fills the lobby. A man comes in, nods and stands behind me. I am reading the post office noticeboard and don't take much notice.

Heavens knows what is going on inside the post office; we have been standing out here forever. Time has ceased to exist. Having now read the notices for community activities, of which there are few and only on Zoom, I bring my attention back to the lobby. The back of my neck begins to prickle. I rub the area through my hood. The prickling continues. Compulsively, I turn around. The man behind me lowers his mask briefly and smiles. It's George.

I feel the anger overwhelm me. "Go away, you maniac," I yell, startling the other lobby occupants. "Leave me alone." They stare at me. George stands behind me, mask in place, saying nothing. Enough. I barge out of the lobby yelling over my shoulder, "I'm going to report you for stalking."

Shaken, I climb back into my car, throwing my purse on the passenger seat. I look back at the post office. He hasn't followed me. Damn the man. Now I still don't know if my books have arrived. What day is it? I look across the square. Ah, there is a line-up outside the Thrift Shop (Covid rules). It must be at least Thursday, Friday or Saturday: those are the days the Thrift Shop is open. I swear, they make more money than any other business in town. All the money goes to the hospital, I believe. I'll go in there and look at the—I call it 'the china rack'; that will pass the time and calm me down.

I join the line-up. Only so many people are allowed inside at one time and we have to sign our names and cleanse our hands first. I recognize no one. I need to get out more; meet new people and stop being a hermit. I'm freezing and my teeth are chattering. I pick up a basket and scurry to the back of the large room; the 'china rack' is located there. So, it appears, are most of the customers. Using my wire basket to good effect, I manage to maneuver myself in front of the racks. I'm on the lookout for egg cups. Why are egg cups so hard to find? There is nothing better than soft-boiled eggs with buttered soldiers. I hear a voice in my head—at least I think it is in my head. 'I saw some over there.' I turn around. It's George again. This is totally the last straw that broke... you know the rest of that saying.

I scream at him. "God damn you, George Freeman. That. Is. It. I am reporting you." I swing the wire basket. It seems to pass right through him and slams instead into the 'china rack'. All hell breaks loose as people stare at me in horror and the entire rack collapses to the ground with a wild clatter and banging of shattered plates, cups, bowls and, no doubt, egg cups. The silence that follows is profound as people stand like frozen statues. (I remember playing a game like that as a child). I take advantage of the still life tableau and force my way out of the shop. Well, that's less profit for the hospital, I guess.

Chapter 14

I run to my car, well, jog really or, to be brutally honest, stagger; I haul myself into the driver's seat and reverse, just missing an oncoming car. I am determined to go to the Police Station. This man will not stalk me anymore. I hope he goes to jail and they throw away the key.

The situation feels surreal. I pull into the Police Station parking lot. Just think, last year, I was dreading any contact with the police. Now I can't wait to talk to them. I walk into the station, see a familiar sign and remember I have no mask on. I go back to the car and realize my purse is resting on the passenger seat along with the car keys. The car doors are all locked.

I begin to sob and return to the station, opening the door. A reinforced glass screen greets me along with a sign: 'Please use the buzzer'. What is the world coming to? Are there no humans left, just signs and buzzers? It's like those automated voices on the phones as you go around and around following the same instructions and never find the centre of the maze. When I worked at a regular job a thousand years ago, I remember being told, when automation was introduced to our phone system, 'we will never leave our clients in the digital parking lot.' Bah humbug.

I hit the buzzer and keep my finger there. A human face appears at the glass screen. An automated-sounding voice says, "alright, I can hear you. You may remove your finger now. How can I help you?"

Tears and snot smear my face. "I've locked my purse and keys in my car."

The automated voice says, "Well, that's not a big deal, dear. Where is your vehicle?"

"Outside, you blithering idiotic dear," I splutter.

The face appears to have a body and the finger attached to that body points to another sign. 'Abusive behaviour will not be tolerated in this building.'

I take a deep breath and grit my teeth. "I apologize. Will

you please phone for someone to come and unlock my car door?"

"That's better, dear. Have a seat while you wait. Do you have funds with you to pay the mechanic?"

I nod, appearing humble, I think. The face disappears. Agh, now I remember why I came here. My finger goes back to the buzzer. I don't leave it there as long this time.

"Sigh—Yes."

"I came here to report something. I need to speak to a policeman?"

"If you promise to be civil, I will assign you to our Community Liaison Officer. He will take your details and assess them for further investigation if required."

I nod my head. I know I must look pathetic but that's good; it will help my cause.

I hear a key turning in a lock. Another door at the side of the little foyer opens.

A man stands there. Thank God he is more than twelve years old.

"Do come in and take a seat," he says, smiling and dangling

a mask in his hand. He is, of course, wearing one. He points to a chair on the other side of a small desk.

Boy, he's a charmer, thirty-ish, blond hair and green eyes. He has a yellow pad in front of him and pulls out a pen.

"My name is Gerry; I am the Community Liaison Officer here. Just so that you are aware, I am not a policeman" he says. "We are contacting someone to retrieve your keys, so you can go ahead and tell me what the problem is. First, please give me your name and contact information."

I do so, sighing deeply and allowing a tear to trickle down my cheek. "I am being stalked," I say dramatically.

His eyebrows raise, but he puts pen to paper. "Who is stalking you? Take your time."

I'll do that alright. "A man called George Freeman. I knew him from the summer market we have here. I am an author and sell my books there. I'm almost famous. My readers often become repeat customers—"

"—George Freeman," he gently interrupts.

"Right. Well, George sells his own canning produce and one day we bought some pickled garlic from him, thinking at the time they were pickled onions, I mean, that's fraudulent behaviour to start with. I'm from England as you can tell from my accent and we love pickled onions and HP sauce…" I see his eyes begin to glaze over.

"Well, the point is, ever since the summer, someone has been sending me pickled garlic cloves and now George is constantly appearing wherever I am and making a nuisance of himself. For example, I was in the Thrift Store just now and he knocked down the entire china stand. I call it 'the china rack'. I know there is no chi…"

"Do you think we can stick to the subject, ma'am," Gerry says with another gentle smile.

I smile back. "Don't call me ma'am; I'm not the bloody Queen," I say and laugh. "I've always wanted to say that. Can you guess who said it?" I beam at Gerry. A frown is now beginning to form on Gerry's forehead. He probably works too hard, poor thing, what with crazy people coming in here day and night and having to deal with all of those druggies as well.

"So," he says with a sigh, "This George Freeman, where does he live?"

"Up the valley somewhere," I say, waving my arms vaguely north. "He must be arrested and put away. He is making my life miserable."

Jerry stands. "I will be back. Please make yourself comfortable."

Our Community Liaison Officer is gone for a long time. I inspect the walls. There is nothing to see but a calendar hanging on one wall, showing, of course, a photo of more mountains topped with snow. I look for my nail file then remember my purse is locked in the car. I hear voices out in the foyer, lobby, whatever. Some other poor soul in need, no doubt.

After what seems like an hour, Gerry returns. I like saying Gerry; it makes us seem like friends and I don't appear to have many if any.

"What you tell me is very interesting," Gerry says. "George Freeman died in August of last year from injuries sustained while at the market in town. The case is still open. I have given your details to Sergeant Cooper who is in charge of this station. Also, there is a woman from the Thrift Shop here to lodge a complaint about a woman who destroyed their property only an hour ago."

I only really take in the first bit. George Freeman died. George Freeman died. How can that be when I see him everywhere and he sends me garlic cloves. Bugger the Thrift Shop, there are more things at stake here, including my sanity.

The door opens. In comes a large RCMP officer, policeman written all over him.

"I'm Sergeant Cooper, ma'am. I just need to ask you a few questions, clarify several issues, alright?"

What, I can say no? Also, I don't repeat my ma'am comment; it didn't seem to break down any barriers before. I shuffle in my chair.

"You stated to our Liaison Officer that you are being stalked by George Freeman and that he, about an hour ago, behaved, shall I say, like a bull in a china shop. As you have now been informed that Mr. Freeman unfortunately died last year, do you wish to alter your story?"

'No," I say, as firmly as my wobbly voice allows. "That man has been hounding me for weeks and sending me pickled garlic cloves; ergo, he cannot be dead, or" —the alternative solution strikes me like a bolt of lightning—I lean forward speaking slowly and dramatically, "someone is impersonating him."

"Do you have any idea who that might be?"

"I have no idea. Surely that is your job to find out. I am the victim here." I sniff, "and at my age, it really is too bad."

"How do you know Mr. Freeman?"

"We were colleagues at the summer market last year. I did hear that he had been attacked but that's all."

"How did you hear that he had been attacked?"

"Oh, everybody knew; it was the talk of the market."

"Interesting." responded the sergeant. "Now I want to take you to another room where you can be more comfortable. I have some colleagues driving up here from our Regional Office. They want to talk to you."

"Make myself comfortable? I just want you to get my car keys out of the car and arrest whomsoever is impersonating George Freeman. What on earth could they possibly want to talk to me about?"

"Unfinished business, I believe."

Chapter 15

Make myself comfortable indeed: a table, four chairs and a large clock on the wall do not comfort make. I sit in that room for an eternity. A minion brings me a cup of weak tea and leaves without speaking. I hear a key turn in the lock as he comes in and when he goes out. I am allowed to use the washroom as needed. Other than that—nothing.

Many hours later, the door opens and in comes a tall man with lank hair, a large bristly chin and a well-worn baggy suit. He reminds me of a crumpled bed. He is followed by a pert blond in a tight blue suit wearing way too much make-up, not that I am judgmental.

"Well, I hear you are our writer from the market," says Bristly Chin as they sit down. "I'm Staff Sergeant Durham and this is Corporal Moore. We are investigators with the Serious Crimes Unit?" They both flash their badges at me. Big deal.

"We are going to record this session. Corporal, please turn on the recorder. Thank you. Present in the room is Staff Sergeant Durham, Corporal Moore and the suspect. Now I understand you told Sergeant Cooper that you knew Mister George Freeman had been attacked. Is that true? Please answer the question for the recorder."

"Yes, So what?"

"I find it interesting as that information was never released to the public. Mr. Freeman was taken by ambulance to our Regional Hospital. He was still alive. Did you know?"

"How would I know? Is that a trick question?"

"Whoever attacked him and callously pushed him under the table, believing him dead—or not—could have saved him, had he or she had the guts to open their mouth."

I say nothing. What can I say? Who is going to believe me if I say I did it because he Didn't. Label. His. Jars.?

"I came here voluntarily to report that I was being stalked and I locked my keys in the car," I say. "I am the victim. The fact that you are questioning me is beyond belief."

"Who is stalking you?"

‘Someone who is impersonating George Freeman,” I almost scream but keep it down a notch or two.

“No need to raise your voice,” says Pertyface. “You told the Liaison Officer here that someone, and you think it is George, has been sending you jars of pickled garlic cloves. Is this true?”

I nod my head.

“Please answer for the tape.”

“Yes,”

“I asked you not to shout, remember.” Pertyface glanced at her notebook. “Isn’t it a coincidence that Mr. Freeman was hit on the head with a jar of pickled garlic cloves, as a result of which, he died of a fractured skull?”

“Nothing to do with me,” I say.

“Well, I do believe we have enough circumstantial evidence to question you further, so, I shall arrange transport to take you to our regional facility. Do you have anyone we need to notify?”

I am in shock. That God damn George has done this to me. I could kill him. When I realize what I just thought, I begin to laugh.

"You find this funny?" Pertyface spoke again.

"My husband should be informed. I gave our phone number to Gerry."

"Interview terminated," says Bristle Chops. He clicks off the machine. "We will see you at Headquarters shortly."

They unlock the door and leave. The door is locked from the other side.

Chapter 16

A short time later, I am brought from the room with no view and taken outside by another large RCMP officer. On the way out of the door, the face behind the glass partition calls out, "I left a message with your husband, on the answering machine, I mean."

So, what's new. God only knows where that man gets to every day. The officer opens the back door of the police car and places a hand as large as a dinner plate on my head and slowly presses down as I step into the car. I have seen this done in so many movies but I never imagined it would happen to me.

"What, no handcuffs?" I say in an attempt at jocularity.

"You haven't been arrested—yet," he says, not so jocularly.

I sit back in the police car and guess they won't be using the – what do they say in British movies – 'blues and twos'. I'm pleased that I am maintaining a sense of humour about this whole farce. Two policemen sit in the front of the car. A mesh screen made of something metallic separates us. Off we go. I turn to look back at my car sitting there, still locked as far as I know, and yelp softly. George is sitting beside me, smiling.

'I thought I would keep you company,' a voice inside my head says. 'Of course, it will only be one way, you won't be coming back again.'

I bang on the mesh. "Help, help, he's here, I told you he was stalking me. Look."

The officer in the passenger seat turns around. "Settle down, ma'am. You are safe here. You have two policemen looking after you." He chuckles and turns back.

I hear him say, "mad as a hatter," to his mate. Then he turns on the police radio, which splutters and hisses.

I bet anything he doesn't know the saying 'mad as a hatter' comes from the time when hat makers in the North of England used mercury as part of the manufacturing process. The resulting mercury poisoning produced hallucinations, depression, memory problems and tremors. Oh, for God's sake, woman, focus.

George turns to me, 'I know you believe you got away with

killing me, but I'm going to make sure you don't, get away with it, I mean.'

"How do you plan to do that, George? You're dead, remember." I whisper this in order to avoid any further comments on my mental state.

'I thought we would move in together. I'll make you lots of pickled garlic cloves. Maybe some pickled onions too.'

"If you think I'm going to live with a ghost, you must be mad." Can ghosts be mad? The only ghosts I'm familiar with are in Dicken's 'A Christmas Carol'. Now that is scary stuff. I mean you never know what they are going to do next.

"Anyway, I'm already married and I don't think Jay would like you hanging around."

'That's what you think.'

"What's that supposed to mean?"

'Ask him next time you see him. Ask him about jars of pickled garlic too.'

"Do go away George and let me live my life."

'That's funny. You wouldn't let me live mine.'

Chapter 17

I finally become aware we are in the city and the police car turns into the gateway of an impressive building with high walls. The driver parks the car. The two policemen get out and one comes to the back and opens the door.

"Jeez, Doug, what did you have for lunch. There sure is a strong smell of garlic in here."

The other policeman looks offended. "Pizza from down the road. What's your beef? It was mainly pepperoni."

"We'd better leave the window open a bit. Air the car out or somebody is gonna complain."

I am escorted into the building by the two big boys. They check in with whoever is on the front desk and off we go to another small room with no view and nothing on the wall to look at.

'Don't worry, I'll keep you company,' says the voice in my

head.

~~We~~ I sit staring at the industrial beige painted walls, trying to ignore the persistent chat from my invisible companion. Eventually, the same two interrogators joins ~~us~~ me.

"Whew. Who was using this room before us? It stinks." says Miss pancake-make-up face.

"Switch on the recorder, let's get this over with." Bristle Chops grunts.

"Present in the room is Staff Sergeant Durham, Corporal Moore and the suspect."

And a ghost, I almost add but bite my tongue just in time.

"We are continuing the conversation we began earlier today," says Bristle Chops.

Miss Pert takes out a notebook as she shuffles a pile of papers in front of her.

A pile of papers? I know that trick. I used it myself in 'Death Does Not Discriminate'.

"Would you mind taking us through your actions on the day in question? I am, of course, referring to the incident at the market last year regarding George Freeman." Bristle Chops, in his shabby brown suit, hair hanging lankly and chin looking like a startled hedgehog, bores holes in me with his eyes.

"Well, of course, I will be glad to. Are you asking everyone these questions and why now after all this time?" I say, knowing police procedure backwards and inside out.

"We ask the questions, ma'am. Please proceed."

I repeated my story of waiting for Jay to bring my coffee and muffin and not seeing the Egg Lady. "I decided to go to the washroom before the doors opened, so to speak."

"Did you engage in conversation with any other stall-holders on your walk to the washroom?" That question came from Miss Pert.

"I speak to everyone," I say, "Good morning, good morning. It's routine."

"Did you say good morning to George Freeman?"

"George Freeman? I'm not sure I know a George Freeman."

'Of course, you knew me. You still know me.'

Cretin.

"I may have said good morning to George, I don't remember. When one is going to the washroom and wants to be back before the visitors are let loose, one has to hurry." I sit back and smile.

Bristle Chops rubs his chin. It sounds like sandpaper on wood. "Earlier today, I deemed it important not to share with you the fact that a new witness has come forward and testified that on the date in question, the 21st of August of last year when Mister George Freeman was brutally attacked with a pickle jar and left for dead, you were seen entering the tent of the victim. What do you have to say?"

I shake my head. "If you mean Peter the artist, I told you he never lifts his head from his sketching. Everyone will vouch for that. It won't wash in court. He is not a good eyewitness. I wouldn't even use it in one of my books."

'One-nil to you,' says the voice in my head.

"No, I do not mean Peter Drake if he is the man to whom you refer. I said this is a new witness, name of Elli Sharpe."

I nearly fall off my seat. He means garden gnome, my friend: my only friend I might add, other than Gerry, the community liaison officer back at our little police station.

"Ms. Sharpe has made a statement that she too was on her

way to the washroom to change into her, shall we say, work clothes when she saw you. She was about to say hello when she noticed your behaviour was odd. You hovered outside the tent of Mister George Freeman, looking undecided. You entered. You did not exit. The next time she saw you were back at your stall and, this is of great significance; *you were wearing a coat.* Now why would that be, I wonder."

"I was cold, for God's sake," I snap.

"I checked the temperature for that time on that day," smirks Pancake-face, "it was already 24 degrees."

'One all' says the voice.

"To continue," says Bristles. "Another credible witness has made a statement to the fact that you reeked of garlic when he returned to your stall and did comment upon the fact at the time."

The blood in my veins turns to ice. There is only one person in the world who could say that.

"Yes, your husband."

'Two to one and out'.

"Be quiet," I snarl.

"To whom do you speak?" squeaks Pancake.

"To whom do you speak. Wow, you must have excelled at English in school. George, of course. He's sitting by my side making a total pest of himself." I've had enough of this tom-foolery.

"You are referring to George Freeman," says Bristlebush.

I nod.

"Please speak for the tape."

"Yes," I yelled.

"Did you kill George Freeman by striking him on the head with a jar of pickled garlic cloves?"

"Yes," I yell.

That, as they say, is that.

Chapter 18

My day in court is, thankfully, brief.

George and I have spent quite a bit of time already in jail. We pass the time pleasantly enough. We watch videos in the main recreation room with the other inhabitants at the special holding area whilst I continue to undergo psych tests. The other week we watched that movie everyone talks about, 'The Queen's Gambit,' so now we play chess constantly. It must look strange to the others in the rec. room as I appear to play both black and white.

I don't care anymore about my circumstances. Jay has gone away with garden gnome, so I'm told by Bristle Chops. He drops in now and again; why he stays in touch, I do not know. I hope the happy couple will be very happy building dressing rooms together. Apparently, he's sold our house and taken the money. We had shared accounts. Don't ever do that. Are you listening? Anyway, if I am to be certified, who cares. I'm better off than Rochester's wife anyway. ('Jane Eyre', right?)

It's interesting. Most people in here are loopy if you know what I mean. You would think they would be lost in their own world but they are always complaining about the stink of garlic. The staff are nice enough, by the way—it's not like 'One Flew Over the Cuckoo's Nest'; do you remember that movie with what's his name?

Mind you, the patients, or inmates as I refer to them, not only complain about the smell of garlic, they complain about everything: the porridge is lumpy, the potatoes are lumpy, the gravy is lumpy, the ice cream is warm. Again, who cares.

So, back to my day in court. I only have to stand and say 'not guilty'. Three experts come onto the stand and say I'm bonkers or words to that effect. Soon everyone in the room is complaining about the smell of garlic. People begin fanning themselves with papers, I smile. George chuckles inside my head. To be honest I can't smell it anymore. I'm immune.

Off we go to a new home. This one has lots of locked doors and doctors in white coats who all seem to have glasses perched on the end of their noses. Having now met most of them, I have decided they are more bonkers than I am. Actually, you see, I am not bonkers. I know George is real, well, not real, but real, really.

We settle in. Apparently, I'm here for the rest of my life due to the fact that I killed George over a mix up between pickled onions and pickled garlic cloves. No one can understand the motivation. When you have the big three, motive, method and opportunity, it's like holding four aces. Yes, I had opportunity and method but the lack of understandable motive leaves them confused. Had anyone lived in England for five minutes they would have understood.

Chapter 19

I have to say, life is good here. We've all been vaccinated against Covid. Hallelujah. However, we still have the same problem of lumpy food. Why, oh why, can't these cooks whip stuff smoothly? They are probably not proper cooks but inmates, or whatever they call us, probably loonies. Or maybe they call us 'people whose wires have become crossed'. The big secret is, we are cocooned against the madness of the world outside. If folk knew, they would be fighting to be declared insane and line up to get a bed in here.

A funny thing happened a few weeks ago. It was the beginning of winter. Not that winter bothers us. I'm nice and cozy in here. I don't have to pretend to want to climb mountains or skate on a frozen lake; I can just cuddle up to George or play chess. And are we getting good at that, and the cuddle, I might mention.

Three of us 'wires crossed folk'—not George and me—three others, had a thriving business selling stuff from their lockers, like shampoo, toothpaste and deodorant, personal supplies brought in by their wives. Well, the three escaped!

It happens now and again, locked wards or not. Maybe bribery was involved. Or whatever.

By the end of the winter (April I think, I lose count), the escapees are back. They'd been pickled up; I mean picked up in Florida. Boy, do they look good, suntanned, healthy, full of Vitamin D.

George and I look at one another. Maybe?

Anyway, I had access to the computers in the library and that's when I got the idea of writing my story. Not any murder story but this story. So, every day, I am permitted to spend two hours in the library typing away. George comes along to add his two cents worth or browse the books. He still liked to read, mainly gardening stuff about garlic, of course. We have become used to the complaints about the smell of garlic everywhere, but we just ignore them.

It takes about two years but I finish the book. I don't really have an ending that I like but I make do with what I have. Maybe the real ending will happen down the road. That's the beauty of computers, there is no beginning and end. What I am trying to say is when I send the manuscript out to agents and publishers, they don't care who I am or where I am. I use a pseudonym anyway.

I snag an agent; publishers love true murder mysteries and this one is a beauty. I am offered a five-figure contract for two books. I take it. Of course, the money goes into a new bank account with my new author's name and life carries on.

Chapter 20

The staff are generally good guys and girls or should I say women, to be politically correct. They sure have a lot to put up with. We are assigned groups every two days: group therapy they call it. My group is quite chatty and, I may proudly boast, literate. We discuss books, yes books. I often drop hints about my book titles but for some reason, the staff don't pick up on it. Not that I would make any money, of course, but you would think they might buy them for the library if they are still available. I do see them listed on Amazon. The question is; do people want to read the work of someone diagnosed as a total psycho who murdered someone over pickles, or not?

George and I carry on with our chess games too, but we are also *making plans.* I will say no more at this point.

There are a few irritations. One guy, Slug Slowly, is in our block. Seriously, this guy moves at a snail's pace, hence his nickname. You do not want to find yourself behind him in the cafeteria. You will not eat. The food, even the lumpy potatoes, will be gone. It's alright for George, he doesn't need to eat, but I do. Remember, I have issues with low blood sugar.

Mention of Slug brings to mind a funny story that we heard via the amazing gossip grapevine that functions here. Slug had an appointment with the dentist in a different block. The poor nurse who had drawn the short straw to take him was walking ahead of him, oh so slooowly. When she turned around, he had vanished. The police found him three blocks away. Way to go, Slug!

There is another irritant here; her name is Winslowe. I mean, Winslowe. Really. I don't know her history but she is one mean SOB. (My language has deteriorated since I came here. I apologize).

Whenever she can make fun of me regarding George, she will. I realize she can't see him, but there he is, and his garlic smell goes with him. I have learned that Winslowe is in here because she chopped somebody up. I don't know any more than that. She certainly has decided I am an easy target.

"How's George today? How's your little pickle juice? Fancy an onion?"

How she knows about the onions, I don't know. Maybe she saw it in the paper; there was a lot of publicity at the time. The Press named it 'The Pickle Jar Murder'. I am keeping my eye on her. So is George.

It all came to a head one day. It was my old nemesis, low blood sugar. Did you ever read Agatha Christie's 'Nemesis'? I loved those stories. She wrote two about Jason Rafael. I digress.

I am standing in the queue at lunchtime. Winslowe is ahead of me in the cafeteria and unfortunately so is Slug. I feel my blood sugar sinking and so many people are ahead of me. George whispers in my ear, 'go to the back of the queue.' I do as George tells me. Winslowe begins yelling at Slug who ignores her. She picks up her tray and hits him over the head with it, hard. In rush the staff who restrain Winslowe. Slug is carried out on a stretcher. The queue vanishes as everyone rushes forward to get an eyeful of the action. I fill my plate and seat myself at an empty table where I hear George's voice. 'Easy-peasy'. The darling is taking care of me.

Winslowe is never seen again in our establishment. She may be in a padded cell for all I know—or care. It occurs to me that she too may have low blood sugar issues. George and I carry on playing chess and attending group therapy.

I told you we had a plan. Well, this is it. We are going to escape. I know I said this is a cocoon but it is full of crazies. When it's time to go then it's time to go. We have money stashed away. My new publisher doesn't know or doesn't care that I am in a crazy hole. He's making lots of money from my first book with him, 'Pickled Onions Matter'.

How to do it is the big question. I have an advantage: George. Ghosts can do things we can't. Cast your mind back again to 'A Christmas Carol'.

The day arrives. Sunday is always the quietest day here with only a skeleton staff in attendance.

We know that the staff change-over is at 3 pm. They gather in the office to give and receive the day's report. George has already removed the spare keys from the rack in the office. Not smart, a key rack in full view.

It is too easy. I walk out. Well, we walk out. We find a car in the parking lot with the doors unlocked. George does something with the wires. Genius. I drive away. Goodbye cocoon.

It's tricky. We can't check into a hotel as we have no identification or money, so we park in a motel parking lot and sleep there. Well, I sleep. George doesn't need to sleep but I feel him cuddling me.

The next day, I slip into a computer centre in a dingy mall. It doesn't take long before I have secured access to my account and contacted my agent. Bribery always pays. For a substantial sum, she will obtain new credentials for me, knowing there is more payout to come with the second book. I am golden once more.

George and I stay in a luxurious hotel until my new papers arrive by courier. George particularly enjoys the sauna and hot tub, never having experienced them before. He doesn't take up much room, I have to say.

The rest of the story doesn't take long. A ticket bought online to… why should I tell you? George doesn't require a seat so one seat will do. As I walk along the long corridor to the plane with George hovering just by my right shoulder, I think of Jay and his garden gnome. I grit my teeth and try to wish them well – but fail. So what; wherever they are, they won't be as happy as George and I are.

Chapter 21

Imagine the turquoise water, with an occasional pod of dolphins leaping. Envisage a blue sky with the occasional puffy cloud—just enough clouds so that I can picture different shapes of animals as I sip on my rose-coloured drink complete with a tiny matching umbrella. George is lying on the hammock beside our pool. He need not fear sun damage whereas I am in the shade of a huge palm tree.

Life is good. Our house, or should I say mansion, sits on the side of a cliff with white steps leading down to our cabana by the sea. I write most mornings and walk on the beach in the afternoons with George. As it is *our* private beach, we do not fear bumping into strangers who may complain of the strong smell of garlic.

George and I fit together like toffee wrapped around a toffee apple. We never argue; he ensures I eat at regular intervals so that I remain his sweet-tempered darling. I know where he is all the time, unlike 'he who shall never be mentioned' along with his popsy gnome.

The money rolls in. It appears that since I became a murderer, my imagination has made a sharp turn toward the darkness. I conceive incredibly bizarre plots with complex villains and naïve suffering victims—so much fun—and my publisher loves them.

Our Saturday Market has become a sepia-tinted memory. I remember the traders there with fondness. Every two weeks, George and I book the little island-hopping plane and visit our new market on the main island. I enjoy observing the traders there and imagine their counterparts back home—or what used to be home. The lady selling local honey and wearing a multi-coloured caftan with a matching turban makes me think of Sandra and her husband who have the honey/bee farm up the valley. Well, I guess they do; it's been a while.

A man with skin the colour of the wood he carves into elaborate dolls makes me think of our pepper pot neighbour and his son who helped us set up the so-called pop-up tent. Over by the ramshackle shed painted in various colourful layers of flaking paint is the stall of Dolores. She has a thriving business selling her homemade rum by the plastic glass or what looks like empty gallon-sized gas containers. I had a sip once. My head almost blew off. I warned George not to sample. I cannot imagine what happens if a ghost's head blows off. Perish the thought. Dolores may not look like Mary of the Vineyard at our old market or our award-winning vodka and gin makers; her black and grey streaked hair hangs down her back in thick ropes entwined with exotic blooms and her laugh is louder than a braying donkey, but I see Mary in her stead.

Fishermen call from their boats, proclaiming their freshly caught wares. George is not partial to fish; he is mainly a garlic fan but I love fish and plan to load up my baskets in preparation for freezing. Fruit and vegetables follow; pineapples, coconuts, papayas, amaranth and bok choy. A hired man follows us around carrying the baskets, which grows fuller and fuller.

This is my new social place, I think with satisfaction. I am feeling both sadness and relief at not having to sell my books at a stall. The market back home used to be my happy place but that locale turned sour for reasons already discussed. Now I enjoy the same bustling atmosphere, the jocularity between traders and a multitude of diverse sights and smells. Speaking of smells; it appears that George still permeates the area with the ripe odour of garlic. As I have said before, I am no longer aware of it but others are. I become aware of strange looks from the traders, usually wrinkling their noses and looking around for the source. Even the fishermen begin to give us puzzled looks as layers of garlic overwhelm the powerful salty tang of the ocean. I say 'us' but of course I mean me; they cannot see the source of the aroma—my sweetie, George.

We head back to the plane followed by our heavily laden man, shopping now complete for a couple of weeks. Our island looks so welcoming as we land on our airstrip. Home again.

Chapter 22

Another perfect day unfolds. I have completed my written word count for the day and George and I are settled in our cabana after our beach walk, drinks in hand—me anyway—and watch the waves roll in. We are playing the old children's game of counting waves and watching them build until number seven, always supposed to be the biggest wave to crash on the shore. The sun is beginning its descent toward another spectacular sunset when I hear the drone of our local plane. I had not booked it and we certainly are not expecting visitors. It must be heading toward a nearby island; perhaps the usual evening breeze has changed directions. I put the distraction out of my mind and sip my sundowner with appreciation. George makes them for me although he never touches a drop. The concoction is amazing: rum from Dolores at the market,

Maraschino Liqueur, Curacao, a splash of lime juice and tonic (only ever Tee-Tree Tonic flown in especially) and a garnish of fresh lime.

How much more perfect can life be?

I am so intent on watching the fiery red sun begin its descent into the ocean (I am totally over the bad effect of red suns) that I don't hear footsteps crunching on the sand.

Two shapes appear before me, cast in shadow and blocking the sun.

"Well. Well, well, if it isn't our almost famous author; except that you are now a famous author."

The familiar voice freezes my bones despite the lingering heat of the tropical evening, Staff Sergeant Durham, no less and the other shape must be… yes, Corporal Pancake-face herself. I shade my eyes so that I can see them better and give myself time to become composed.

"What an unexpected pleasure." I laugh, proud of my firmness of voice. "What brings you to our little island? George, we have guests."

"George is still with you then?" Bristle Chin enquired,

looking more like a well-loved dog's blanket than ever.

"But of course. Why would he not be? We are as Darby and Joan, Laurel and Hardy, Martin and Lewis; bound together as one."

I turn my gaze to Miss Perky but something is different. Gone is the dark blue 'I am a female investigative police officer and must wear this navy-blue suit'. Instead, she has donned a frilly blouse and a long, swinging floral skirt. Something is not jibing here.

"George, pour our guests a glass of your sundowner. On the other hand, I will. Pull up a chair and do tell how you found us."

Bristle Chin and Perky make themselves comfortable and take a sip of their rum. The expression on their faces is almost worth seeing them again—but not quite.

After he has recovered from a major choking attack, Bristle Chops clears his throat. "It wasn't hard, me being a detective an' all. I had started reading your old books and enjoyed noting all of your police procedural errors."

I growled. Not funny.

He continued. "I actually became more interested in reading, something I hadn't done for years."

Tell me about it, I thought, remembering all of the blank faces at the market when I asked what they enjoyed reading.

"So, I started searching for other authors at the library and found one I really enjoyed. Not only that, the murder case reminded me of yours. When the author's new books came out, I would be sure to read them. I finally realized the two authors were one and the same. The plots were nastier—how do you come up with such horrors—but the style was the same. Bingo! You were writing under a pseudonym.

"I contacted your publisher and your agent, waving my badge around. They said they had no idea where you were. I, shall we say, encouraged them to reveal where your cheques were being deposited—an off-shore island no less, was the final resting place."

"All very interesting," I said, "but that doesn't get you here."

"True, but the information put me in the vicinity. We decided to explore the islands in this archipelago as your cheques are deposited on the main island. By the way, we have tied the knot, taken the plunge, married, so meet Mrs. Petunia Durham."

A little flag raised its head once I absorbed the name. Petunia! "Mrs. Durham, not Corporal Durham?" I ask, hope rising in my breast.

"We decided to keep this information about your location to ourselves. Petunia and I were ready for retirement anyway; we had both done our time saving the Nation from criminal types such as yourself."

I glare at him.

Mr. Durham continues. "We began hearing rumours of a strange phenomenon on one of the islands; a strong smell of garlic was occasionally invading the area, causing the locals some distress. It only took a few questions to discover that an eccentric old lady flies in to shop at the market using the local taxi plane and her visits always coincide with the garlic odour. A word with the pilot and—here we are!

Eccentric old lady indeed. "Very clever, I grunt, "You've answered 'how' but now the question becomes 'why'?"

Bristle Chin settles more comfortably into his chair and risks a tiny sip of his drink.

"As I said, we are retired but not on full pensions. We need to bulk them up quite a bit and we thought we might enjoy living on a small, private island. I think we could become used to the smell of garlic and might even enjoy playing a round of cards or a game of chess with you and George. Oh, by the way, I bumped into your former husband and invited him and his wife to join us, if they so desired. I thought it was the least you could do after your treatment of him. However, if you choose not to accept our company, we'll inform the authorities of your whereabouts."

There you have it. Life goes on as usual; I write, walk the beach with George, enjoy sundowners with Clarence—yes, Clarence, I know it's hard to believe—and Petunia. Every two weeks we all climb into the tiny plane and explore the main island market together. One day, I may hear the drone of our little plane bringing more guests to the party.

Who would have thought a murder at a Farmers' and Artisans' Market caused by a combination of garlic cloves along with a craving for pickled onions, a red sun and low blood sugar would have brought together our new eclectic ménage: a famous author, a crooked ex-cop and his equally crooked mate along with a sweety-pie ghost called George, all living harmoniously on this enchanted, aromatic isle?

ACKNOWLEDGEMENTS

My husband is the inspiration behind this book. Every Saturday he supported my endeavours at the market and repeatedly said, "You should write a book about the market." I'm not sure he expected this one.

I wish to acknowledge my early readers who are excellent at giving their honest feedback:

Karen Sharp, Ralph Brade, (my foreign correspondent) and Bruce Robinson. I offer a special shoutout to Bruce who has helped immensely with readability.

Many thanks to our local RCMP for guidance on police matters. Any errors are my own.

Finally, grateful thanks are extended to Shawn Wernig of eggplantstudios.ca for answering all of my many questions promptly and for keeping me afloat technically.

When I told some of the traders that I was planning a book about our market but I would not use real names; they all said, "Please put my name in". So, with their permission, here is a list of some of the traders mentioned in the story:

Jay – Jim Fisher (not a trader, my real sweetie)

Claire and Dave Carter - rockymtnhoneyfarm@gmail.com

Chris@tayntonbayspirits.com

Egg Lady - Mary-Lou Flegel of the Royal Canadian Legion, Branch 71

Tom and Dan – Ken Carlow and Marius Hoofd: Market Management Team, Royal Canadian Legion, Branch 71

Margaret Basaraba - wynnwoodcellars@gmail.com

Angela Ross - valleylifedesigns@gmail.com

The Pepper Mill Guys - Sean and Mitchel Mathews - tracyfineproducts@gmail.com

Emma Stephens (garden gnome) - info@untamedfernie.com who is definitely not passed her prime.

Stephen Pavey- spavey6@hotmail.com - Cascading Mini Donuts

Patrick Yesh - Artist - Art Heart and Soul.com

George – Reg Jegges - Reg does label his garlic pickle jars.

Also, please be reminded that ‘Murder At The Market’ is Fiction. All of the people above had nothing to do with the story. Really!